IN THE
MAGIC
CORRIDOR

STORIES FOR
WHOLE LANGUAGE LEARNING

HOLLY L. EUBANKS

ILLUSTRATED BY
ANN C. CHAPIN

Dominie Press, Inc.

Publisher: Raymond Yuen

Executive Editor: Carlos Byfield

Project Editor: Liz Parker

Cover and Text Illustrator: Ann C. Chapin

Text Design: Siri Johansson

Dominie Press, Inc.
5945 Pacific Center Boulevard
San Diego, California 92121

ISBN 1-56270-043-X

Printed in USA

2 3 4 5 6 7 8 9 W 98 97 96 95 94 93 92

DEDICATION

To our mother and father, both teachers,
from whom we learned so much.

CONTENTS

ONE GOOD TURN DESERVES ANOTHER

eopard walked along in the jungle. Suddenly, he fell into a
trap.

No matter how hard he tried, he could not get out. He began to cry for help.

Man was walking in the jungle also. He heard the cries. Following the sound, he came to the trap. He looked down into
the pit, and there was Leopard.

"Help me, Man!" cried Leopard. "If you help me, I will be your friend
forever."

"No, you won't," answered Man. "You will eat me. I know you."

Leopard looked very surprised. "I wouldn't do that," he said. "I would
never eat anyone who saved my life."

Man thought about that and decided to help Leopard. But as soon as
Leopard was out of the pit, he grabbed Man.

"Now I am going to eat you," he said. "I am very hungry."

"But you promised that if I helped you, you would not," said Man.

"Well, so I did," said Leopard. "So this is what I will do. We will have a
trial. I will call a jury of three animals. If any one of them will say that there
is goodness in man, you will live. If not, you will die."

Horse, Cow, and Monkey arrived. Leopard called upon Horse first. "Is
there any goodness in the heart of man?" he asked.

"No," answered Horse, "there is not. Men have used us when they had

"What is so funny?" asked Leopard. "What are you laughing about?"

strength of their own. When we became old, they turned us out to die. I say eat the man."

"And Cow, what do you say?" asked Leopard.

"I agree with Horse," said Cow. "Men care only about what we can give them. When we are no longer useful, they kill us and eat us. They give our bones to their dogs. I say eat the man."

Leopard then turned to Monkey. Monkey had begun to laugh.

"What is so funny?" asked Leopard. "What are you laughing about?"

"I can't understand how anyone as smart as Man could fall into his own trap," said Monkey.

"No, you idiot, it wasn't Man who fell into the trap. It was I," said Leopard.

Monkey hopped over to the pit and looked in. Then he looked up at Leopard. He started to laugh again, harder and harder. He rolled on the ground and held his sides, laughing all the while.

"Stop that!" ordered Leopard. "This is not funny! What are you laughing at now?"

"YOU!" chattered Monkey. "You could never fit in that pit! You are much too big." And he laughed some more.

Leopard now was quite angry. He jumped up, stalked over to the pit, and leaped in.

"There! Now do you see?" growled Leopard.

But Monkey did not answer. He turned to Man and said, "Next time, don't listen to promises made by leopards." And as he swung away through the trees he called, "And always remember that one good turn deserves another!"

ANOTHER GOOD TURN

Building Reading Comprehension

Answer the questions. Use complete sentences. Look back at the story if you need help.

1. Who walked along in the jungle?

   _____

2. Where did Leopard fall?

   _____

3. What did Leopard want Man to do?

   _____

4. What promise did Leopard make to Man?

   _____

5. Did Leopard keep his promise? Why or why not? What excuse did he give?

   _____

   _____

6. Who was on the jury?

   _____

7. What did Horse and Cow have to say about Man?

   _____

   _____

8. How did monkey trick Leopard?

   _____

   _____

FOR GOODNESS' SAKE

Building Story Interpretation

The horse and the cow said there is no goodness in man. Do you agree or disagree? State your case. Give evidence to support your position.

_____

_____

_____

_____

_____

_____

_____

_____

_____

_____

_____

_____

_____

_____

WHAT'S THE VERDICT?

Building Creative Thinking

Write on one of the following topics:

- Leopard is trapped for the second time in the pit. He is trying to persuade Man to let him out again. What does he say?

- Is it fair to pick your own jury? Explain.

- Monkey never does take a position about goodness in the heart of man. What do you think he thinks? What would his answer have been?

- What is one of the lessons of this story?

- "One good turn deserves another" is a popular saying. What do you think it means? How does it fit in this story?

- Here are some other popular sayings. What do you think they mean?

  "Every dog has his day"

  "Live and let live"

  "A fool and his money are soon parted"

  "Better half a loaf than none"

  "Sly as a fox"

I WOULD IF I COULD

Building Grammar and Syntax

Study these sentences. Discover the rule.

> If I have time, I will go tomorrow.
> If he studies hard, he will do well on his test.
> What will you do if you win the lottery?
> What will we do if it rains?

> If I had time, I would go. (But I don't have time.)
> If he had studied, he would have passed the test. (But he didn't.)
> If he drove the speed limit, he would not get so many tickets.
> If he ate properly, he would feel better.

- *If the verb in the* if *clause is in the present tense, use* will.
- *If the verb in the* if *clause is in the past tense, use* would.

Complete each sentence with will *or* would.

1. If he is not careful, Leopard _____ fall into the trap.

2. Leopard _____ get out if he could.

3. If Leopard asked Man, _____ Man help?

4. If you were Man, _____ you help Leopard escape?

5. If Leopard had put men on the jury, the trial _____ have been more fair.

6. What _____ Leopard do if Man tried to run away?

7. If Leopard falls into another trap, he _____ probably ask Monkey to help him.

8. If Man is smart, he _____ not help leopards in traps.

9. Do you think Man _____ help Leopard a second time?

10. If you knew someone with a problem, _____ you help?

7

A GAGGLE OF GEESE

Building Vocabulary

Groups of animals have their own special names. Match the group name with the animals that fit. Use your dictionary to help you. Some group names go with more than one kind of animal.

1. _____ a gaggle	**a.** of whales
2. _____ a pod	**b.** of wolves
3. _____ a pride	**c.** of geese
4. _____ a pack	**d.** of sheep
5. _____ a flock	**e.** of horses
6. _____ a herd	**f.** of lions
7. _____ a school	**g.** of bees
8. _____ a covey	**h.** of kittens
9. _____ a swarm	**i.** of cattle
10. _____ a crowd	**j.** of birds
11. _____ a brood	**k.** of quail
12. _____ a litter	**l.** of flies
13. _____ a colony	**m.** of fish
	n. of elephants
	o. of ants
	p. of chicks
	q. of dogs
	r. of people

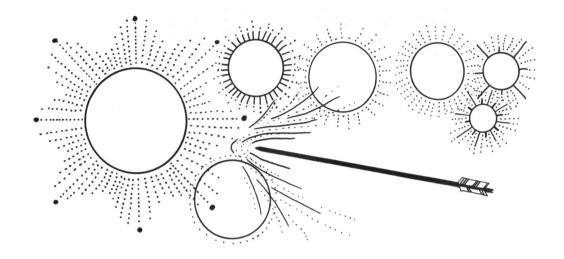

SEVEN SUNS

n olden times, there was not just one sun in the sky. There were seven, and they all burned bright and hot. There was no night in those times. There was only the bright, hot day. Lao Fu was a fencemaker. He made good strong fences from bamboo poles. Hou Yi was his son. Everyone said that Hou Yi was special. Everyone said that one day Hou Yi would do something wonderful for his village. But Hou Yi did not listen to the townspeople. He did not care about what they said. He liked only to be with his father. He liked the bamboo. And the bamboo liked Hou Yi.

Hou Yi cut himself a pole. It was young and green and strong. He cut a notch in each end, and strung a piece of cord tightly through each notch.

"What a fine bow!" said Hou Yi's father. "What will you shoot?"

"I will shoot the suns out of the sky," said Hou Yi, laughing.

Lao Fu watched as his son made beautiful arrows from young bamboo. He watched as his son climbed the tallest mountain in the land. He watched as Hou Yi began to shoot the arrows at the suns.

All of the townspeople began to laugh at Hou Yi. "He has gone mad," they said to Lao Fu. "You must take his bow. You must hide his arrows. Send him to school. Send him away from here."

But Lao Fu paid no attention to the townspeople. Day after day he watched his son shoot arrows at the suns. Every day he said, "Today your arrows traveled faster and farther. Shoot again tomorrow."

When it hit, the sun popped like a balloon and fell from the sky.

One day, one of Hou Yi's arrows flew all the way to one of the suns. When it hit, the sun popped like a balloon and fell from the sky. The earth grew cooler, and for the first time there were shadows.

All of the townspeople were amazed. They stopped laughing. They began to watch Hou Yi carefully.

The next day Hou Yi shot down another sun. For the first time there was twilight, but there was still no night.

When the third sun fell, the dawn appeared. There was still no night.

When the fourth and fifth suns fell, night appeared. For the first time the townspeople saw the stars in the heavens.

When the sixth sun fell, the moon appeared. The night was twelve hours long.

The townspeople became very afraid. They went to Lao Fu. They bowed and said, "We salute your son. He is the greatest archer the world has ever known. Seven suns were too many. They hid the night and the stars and the moon. But with no suns our world will be in darkness. Talk to Hou Yi. Tell him to stop. Tell him to leave us one sun."

Lao Fu went to his son. "You are a fine son," he said. "And all the people can see that you are the greatest archer in the land. But you must stop shooting the suns. If you shoot down the last one, how will I see to cut my bamboo? Leave us one sun." Hou Yi put down his bow. He walked with his father into the thick bamboo. The two of them were never seen again.

HOW DID IT GO?

Building Reading Comprehension

Below is a short summary of the story. Some of the sentences are true, and some are false. Underline the sentences that are false. Then rewrite the story. Change the sentences that are false. Make them true.

Long ago, there were three suns in the sky. They all burned brightly. In those times, night was short.

Lao Fu was a fisherman. His son, Hou Yi, was an archer.

Hou Yi made himself a wooden bow. He made arrows out of bamboo. He went down into the valley, and began to shoot his arrows at the suns. The townspeople all laughed at Hou Yi. Lao Fu laughed at his son, too. He decided to send Hou Yi away to school.

But Hou Yi kept shooting arrows at the suns. The people kept laughing. One day, one of the arrows hit the moon, and the moon fell from the sky. Then the people stopped laughing.

Hou Yi shot all of the suns out of the sky except one. And since that time, we have both night and day.

_____

_____

_____

_____

_____

_____

_____

_____

_____

OUR HERO!

Building Story Interpretation

The townspeople build a monument to honor Hou Yi. You are to write the events of Hou Yi's life and how the people feel about him. What you write will become the inscription on the statue.

THE BALLAD OF HOU YI

Building Creative Thinking

Choose one of the following activities:

- Write a song or poem telling about the great deeds of Hou Yi.

- Write what a world would be like that had no sun at all.

- Did the story end how you thought it would? Why or why not?

- How else could the story have ended? Write the next episode.

IT HAPPENED JUST THE WAY I SAID IT DID!

Building Grammar and Syntax

Look at the sentences. Discover the rule.

> Today I walk. Yesterday I walked.
> Today you talk. Yesterday you talked.
> Today he listens. Yesterday he listened.

Look at these sentences. You cannot discover the rule.

> Today I begin. Yesterday I began.
> Today you are. Yesterday you were.
> Today he says. Yesterday he said.

Fill in the correct past tense form for each verb in parentheses.

1. Many years ago there _____ seven suns in the sky. *(be)*

2. Lao Fu always _____ good, strong fences. *(make)*

3. The people in the village _____ that Hou Yi would be a great man someday. *(say)*

4. Hou Yi _____ his bow with a piece of strong cord. *(string)*

5. The townspeople _____ to laugh at Hou Yi. *(begin)*

6. Hou Yi practiced until one of his arrows _____ all the way to the sun. *(fly)*

7. The arrow _____ the sun. *(hit)*

8. The sun _____ from the sky. *(fall)*

9. When Hou Yi _____ the sun from the sky, the people

   _____ amazed. *(shoot, be)*

WHO'S ON FIRST?
WHAT'S ON SECOND?

Building Vocabulary

Words for counting numbers go like this:

one, two, three, four, five, six, seven, eight, nine, ten

Words for numbers that show place in line are like this:

first, second, third, fourth, fifth, sixth, seventh, eighth . . .
tenth, eleventh, twelfth, thirteenth, fourteenth, fifteenth . . .
twentieth, thirtieth, fortieth, fiftieth, sixtieth . . .
twenty-first, thirty-second, forty-third, fifty-fourth, sixty-fifth, seventy-
sixth, eighty-seventh, ninety-ninth . . .

The numbers look like this:

1st 2nd 3rd 4th 5th 6th 7th 8th 9th 10th 11th 12th 13th
14th 15th 16th 17th 18th 19th 20th 21st 22nd 23rd 24th
25th 26th 27th 28th 29th 30th 31st 32nd 33rd 34th . . .
41st 42nd 43rd 44th . . .

Write words for each number.

16th _____   4th _____

41st _____   12th _____

82nd _____   25th _____

53rd _____   8th _____

98th _____   60th _____

39th _____   5th _____

67th _____   70th _____

GOOD NEWS
OR BAD?

n old man had seven sons. Six were grown, and had gone into the world to live their own lives. Only the seventh remained at home with his father.

"Tch, tch, tch," clucked the neighbors. "You are an old man. All your sons should be at home to help you. They are selfish boys. What a shame, what a shame!"

"Who can say," answered the old man quietly, "what is a shame and what is not?"

"The old fool," whispered the neighbors. "He understands nothing at all about life."

The next month the neighbors looked out their windows. They watched in surprise as the old man and his son moved to a nearby farm.

"Where are you going?" they asked.

"To my farm," answered the old man.

"To your farm? How did you get this farm?" asked the neighbors enviously.

"My sons are doing well. They bought me this farm. They bought me a horse, too." The old man pointed to a sleek stallion, tied to the gate.

"My, my!" declared the neighbors. "What good news! What good fortune! You are so lucky!"

"So it seems," replied the old man. "But who is to say what is good fortune and what is bad?"

"The old fool," muttered the neighbors crossly. *"He does not understand anything at all."*

"The old fool," muttered the neighbors crossly. "He does not understand anything at all."

The man and his son became farmers. But their lives did not become easier. The farmland was dry and full of rocks. The two had to work hard from sunrise until sunset. They had only the horse to help them. And one day the horse ran away.

"What bad news!" said the neighbors when they found out. "This is terrible. What bad luck!"

The old farmer shrugged his shoulders. "Who knows if the luck is bad or good," he replied.

"The old fool is crazy," said the neighbors. "He does not understand his own life."

Several weeks later, the horse returned from the mountains. He galloped proudly toward the farm. Behind him followed six beautiful wild mares. The farmer's son rounded them up.

"How wonderful!" cried the neighbors. "What good luck!"

"Good luck? Bad luck? Who knows?" said the old man.

A few days later the farmer's son was trying to break one of the horses. The horse bucked and kicked wildly. Off from the horse's back flew the young man. He hit the ground hard and broke his leg.

"We are sorry to hear this terrible news!" exclaimed all the neighbors.

The next week the army marched through the village.

"We need your son to help fight in the war," said the captain to the old farmer.

The old man led the soldier to his son's bedside. The soldier looked at the young man's leg. He turned to the old man and said, "You are in luck. This boy is of no use to us at all." He left the farmer's son at home.

Good news or bad?

OUT OF ORDER

Building Reading Comprehension

These events from the story are in the wrong order. Number them in the correct order.

   3   The old man and his son moved to a farm.

   6   The boy broke his leg.

   2   The neighbors said all the sons should be at home.

   5   The farmer's horse returned with six wild mares.

   7   The army came to town.

   4   The farmer's horse ran away.

   8   The captain left the farmer's son at home.

   1   Six of the farmer's sons went into the world to live their own lives.

GOSSIP

Building Story Interpretation

You are one of the farmer's nosy neighbors. You just can't imagine how his six sons got their money. Write a letter to one of your other neighbors. Spread as many rumors as you can think of about how the boys came into that money.

_____
(date)

Dear _____,

_____

_____

_____

_____

_____

_____

_____

_____

_____

_____

Yours truly,

_____
(your name)

FIRST THINGS FIRST

Building Creative Thinking

Write on any one of the following themes:

- Think of something that happened to you or someone you know that seemed bad at the time but turned out good.

- Imagine you broke your leg. Write a letter to a friend or relative. Tell how the accident had some unexpected good results.

- What happens next in the story?

Here is a list of popular sayings. Some of them could be used in place of the title "Good News or Bad?" Choose the one you think best fits the story. Circle it. Now write about the saying. Why did you choose it? What does it mean to you?

"There's always a light at the end of the tunnel"
"Haste makes waste"
"Tomorrow is another day"
"The grass is greener on the other side"
"First things first"
"Every cloud has a silver lining"
"All's well that ends well"
"Luck be a lady"
"The sun will rise again"
"You scratch my back, I'll scratch yours"
"Here today, gone tomorrow"
"He who laughs last laughs best"
"The longest journey begins with one step"
"Any port in a storm"
"You can't judge a book by its cover"
"A stitch in time saves nine"
"What goes up must come down"
"Don't look a gift horse in the mouth"
"One man's medicine is another man's poison"
"Don't cry over spilt milk"

Building Grammar and Syntax

Action words (verbs) have three parts. These parts are called present tense, past tense, and past participle.

Here are the principle parts of some verbs from the story. Look at the verbs. Discover the rule. Then fill in the blanks with the correct form.

Present Tense	Past Tense	Past Participle
*Am	*was	*been
*Are	*were	*been
grow	*grew	*grown
go	*went	gone
cluck	clucked	_____
_____	whispered	whispered
look	_____	looked
watch	watched	_____
buy	*bought	*bought
_____	pointed	pointed
reply	_____	replied
mutter	muttered	_____

What do you notice?

With most verbs, add -ed to the end to form past tense or past participle.

*Verbs with * break the rule. You must memorize those.*

IT'S ALL
WELL AND GOOD

Building Vocabulary

Study these sentences. Discover the rule. Be able to explain the rule to your partner or group.

The man spoke quietly.	He was a quiet man.
The horse ran swiftly.	It was a swift horse.
The cook worked noisily.	He was a noisy cook.

Write the story. Fill in the blanks with one of the words from the list. You may use some words more than once.

young happy/happily rapid/rapidly tired/tiredly slow/slowly
quiet/quietly quick/quickly careful/carefully old wild/wildly
awful/awfully short/shortly strong/strongly tricky many

A _____ man walked _____

down the road. He came to a river.

"Do you want a ride?" called a _____ boatman.

"Yes, I do!" answered the man _____ .

In the middle of that _____ river, the boatman

stopped rowing.

"My hands are cramping _____ ," he cried out in

pain. "Row us _____ to the bank.

The young man was _____ . He rowed

_____ to the opposite bank. The boatman jumped out

and ran _____ down the road.

And the _____ man rowed the boat for

_____ months to come.

LITTLE
BURNT FACE

ar in the North was a great wide bay. Along its shores lived the tribe of Strong Wind. Strong Wind was a mighty warrior. His bravery was known throughout the land. His people loved him. His enemies feared him.

Strong Wind had a strange and wonderful power. He could make himself as light as an eagle's feather and as invisible as the wind. He would float through the air into his enemies' camps and listen to their plans. Never was Strong Wind's tribe surprised by an attack.

Strong Wind had a sister named White Feather. They lived together in a teepee beside the great bay. White Feather helped her brother in all his work. One day he went to her and said, "My sister, the time has come for me to take a wife. But I will have only a maiden with a truthful heart. You must help me find her."

Many maidens wanted to marry Strong Wind. Many tried to win him. But not one succeeded. Strong Wind's sister gave each maiden a test. To each one she said, "Come tonight at sundown. He comes home at that time. If you can see him, you will become his wife."

Each evening at sunset the maidens arrived. Strong Wind's sister took them down to the beach. She asked them, "Can you see him?" And each maiden answered that she could. White Feather then knew that the girl was lying. White Feather alone could see him.

Now, in the village lived a great chief. His wife had died many years

"Look again," said White Feather. "Look carefully. What do you see?"

before. He had three daughters. As young girls they had been sweet and lovely. As maidens they had become as beautiful as the morning sun. The youngest daughter was more beautiful than words could tell. Her skin was as soft as a fawn's breath. Her hair was as black as a raven's wing. And because she had a gentle heart, all in the village loved her.

But her two sisters were jealous of her beauty. They were cruel to her and gave her only ugly rags to wear. One day, when their father was away from the village, they cut off her hair. They put bee's wax on it so it stuck up in spikes. Then they took hot coals from the fire and burned her face. When their father returned, they said to him, "Father, see what our stupid sister has done! She has ruined herself. You must send her away."

But the chief loved his daughter and would not send her away. She stayed in the tribe. The people gave her the name "Little Burnt Face."

The day came when the chief's two oldest daughters decided to win Strong Wind. They went to White Feather and said, "We will try."

"Come with me," she said. She led them to the beach.

After a while White Feather called out. "Ah," she said, "here he comes." She pointed with her finger towards the ocean. "Do you see him?"

"Oh, yes, there, there!" cried the sisters, pointing to the same spot.

But they were lying, because Strong Wind was standing invisible by his sister's side.

"He is pulling his canoe," said White Feather. "Of what material is the cord?"

"Rawhide," the two sisters answered.

"No, it is not," said White Feather. "You must go. You have failed the test."

The girls went home, angry and embarassed.

Months passed. The chief's youngest daughter thought to herself, "No one has won Strong Wind. All the maidens in the village have tried, all except me. I will try. I may fail. But *not* to try would be my greatest failure."

So she patched her tattered clothes. She put on the little bit of jewelry she owned and started out.

Her sisters laughed at her. "You are an idiot," they jeered. "Strong Wind will not want you. You are too ugly."

Little Burnt Face ignored their insults and went silently on her way.

She came to Strong Wind's tent. His sister waited outside.

"Come, let us walk along the beach," said White Feather. "We will wait together for my brother to come home."

They watched as the sun sank slowly into the ocean. Suddenly, White Feather called out, "Oh, look there! I see him coming now. Do you see him?"

"No," answered Little Burnt Face. "I do not."

"Look again," said White Feather. "Look carefully. What do you see?"

Little Burnt Face looked long and hard. Finally she cried out, "I *do* see him coming! I see him, and he is wonderful!"

"What does he pull?" asked White Feather.

"He pulls a canoe," answered Little Burnt Face.

"Of what is the cord made?" asked White Feather.

Little Burnt Face began to tremble. "I am afraid to say," answered Little Burnt Face.

"Say!" said Strong Wind's sister.

"He pulls the canoe with the rainbow," whispered Little Burnt Face.

"Does he carry anything over his shoulder?" asked White Feather.

"Yes, his bow," said Little Burnt Face.

"Of what is the bow string made?" asked White Feather.

"It . . . it is the Milky Way," said Little Burnt Face.

White Feather took Little Burnt Face by the hand. "Don't be afraid," she said. "You have seen Strong Wind. Come with me to the tent."

She took Little Burnt Face back to the teepee. She bathed her, and Little Burnt Face's scars disappeared. She combed her hair with an abalone shell. Little Burnt Face's hair grew long and black like a raven's wing. She dressed her in fine robes. She gave her rich bracelets and necklaces to wear.

Soon Strong Wind came in. He led Little Burnt Face to the wedding circle in the village. Little Burnt Face sat in the wife's seat. Strong Wind sat beside her. The two were married. Together, they did many brave and wonderful deeds for their tribe.

And what about the two sisters? They were very angry and jealous when they heard that Little Burnt Face had married Strong Wind. They plotted to kill their sister. But Strong Wind learned of their plan. He used his great power to turn the two sisters into aspen trees.

To this day the aspen shivers and shakes when the slightest breeze passes through. It remembers Strong Wind's power and anger so many years ago.

DID IT HAPPEN?
TRUE OR FALSE?

Building Reading Comprehension

Here are some statements about the story you just read. Some of the statements describe things that really happened, and some do not. If the statement is correct, write true *on the line. If it is incorrect, write* false. *Look back at the story if you need help.*

_____ **1.** Strong Wind was the chief of his tribe.

_____ **2.** Strong Wind had no enemies.

_____ **3.** White Feather gave the maidens a test. This was to see if they were honest.

_____ **4.** From the story, we can tell that the chief had both sons and daughters.

_____ **5.** Little Burnt Face had fallen into a bed of hot coals.

_____ **6.** Little Burnt Face had three sisters.

_____ **7.** Strong Wind could make himself invisible.

_____ **8.** From the story, we can tell that Strong Wind discovered the war plans of other tribes.

_____ **9.** The chief had three daughters. Two of them were ugly and one was beautiful.

_____ **10.** Burnt Face's sisters tried to drive her from the village.

_____ **11.** The chief's two oldest daughters went to live with Strong Wind.

_____ **12.** From the story, we know that White Feather is married.

_____ **13.** Little Burnt Face saw Strong Wind pulling a sled.

_____ **14.** Strong Wind's bow string was the rainbow.

REWARD!

Building Story Interpretation

Strong Wind's enemies know he sneaks into their camp and steals their war plans. They don't know how he does it and they have never been able to catch him. They are offering a reward for his capture.

Give any information you can that might lead to Strong Wind's capture. What does he look like? Where has he been seen? How does he get from place to place? (By horse, by boat, on foot?) How could you get him to come out of hiding? How could you lay a trap for him? Work in teams, in groups, or by yourself.

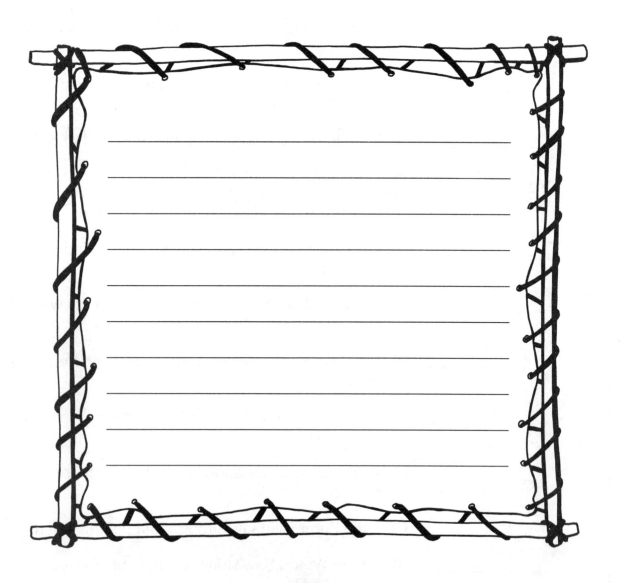

HOW DID IT HAPPEN?

Building Creative Thinking

On your own paper, write a paragraph on three of the following questions:

1. How did Strong Wind get his name?

2. What happened to Strong Wind's sister after he married Little Burnt Face?

3. Little Burnt Face needs a new name. If you were Strong Wind, what name would you give her? Why?

4. Do you like the name your parents gave you? Why or why not? If you could choose any other name, what would it be? Make up an Indian name for yourself. Have the name describe something you do well or like to do.

5. Little Burnt Face's sisters were turned into trees. Imagine they can still talk. Have them describe what it feels like to be a tree.

6. How can you tell when someone is lying?

7. Has anyone ever lied to you? What were their reasons for doing so? How did you feel? Did you punish the other person, or did you forgive him or her?

8. Have you ever lied to anyone? What were your reasons for doing so? Did you get caught? Were you punished? How did the other person feel? Were you forgiven?

9. Talk about a time when lying might be the right choice to make.

10. What is the difference between not telling the whole truth and lying?

11. In the story, was Strong Wind's punishment of the two sisters fair? Why or why not? What would you have done?

12. What is the one most important thing you would look for in a husband or a wife?

BETTER THAN ANYTHING

Building Grammar and Syntax

Study these examples.

> Mad Dog is a warrior. He is brave.
> Scarface is another warrior. He is braver than Mad Dog.
> Strong Wind is also a warrior. He is the bravest of all.

Brave *and* braver *are comparative forms of adjectives.*
Bravest *is the superlative form of the adjective.*

- *Add -er to one-syllable adjectives to show the comparative form.*
- *Add -est to one-syllable adjectives to show the superlative form.*
- *Comparative adjectives are followed by the word* than.
- *Superlative adjectives are preceded by the word* the.
- *Good and* bad *break the rule, so:* good,   better,   best
  bad,   worse,   worst

Complete these sentences. Change the word in parentheses to its comparative form. Don't forget to use the word than.

1. Strong Wind is _____ _____ Scarface. *(brave)*

2. The bay is _____ _____ the lake. *(big)*

3. The chief was _____ _____ the other warriors. *(wise)*

4. White Feather was _____ _____ the two sisters. *(smart)*

5. A breeze is _____ _____ a wind. *(soft)*

6. An aspen tree is _____ _____ a cherry tree. *(tall)*

7. Little Burnt Face's hair was _____ _____ a raven. *(black)*

8. The sun is _____ _____ the moon. *(bright)*

9. Your father is _____ _____ you. *(old)*

10. The test was _____ _____ the maidens thought. *(hard)*

IT'S AS EASY AS PIE

Building Vocabulary

Some comparisons use as . . . as *with an adjective or an adverb, like this:*

Her eyes are as blue as the sky.
It is as loud as a jet engine.
He runs as quickly as a deer.

Write sentences with as . . . as *comparisons using the groups of words given.*

1. Strong Wind / brave / lion

   _____

2. White Feather / tall / tree

   _____

3. skin / soft / silk

   _____

4. Strong Wind / light / feather

   _____

5. hair / black / raven's wing

   _____

6. maidens / beautiful / morning sun

   _____

7. Little Burnt Face / gentle / lamb

   _____

8. sisters / wicked / witches

   _____

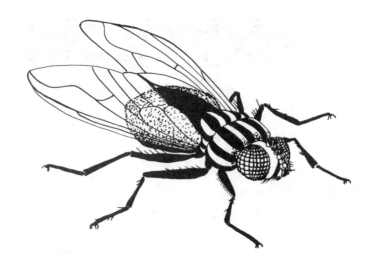

THE
WITNESS

n a certain village lived a moneylender. Everyone knew him, even the little children. No one liked him, not even the dogs.

The moneylender was very, very rich. He made his money by lending money to the poor. He charged the highest interest he possibly could. When his debtors could not pay, he took whatever they had that was valuable. He took their horses, their cows, or even their houses.

A poor fisherman lived in the village. He had borrowed money from the moneylender and had not paid it all back. He wanted to pay, though, and worked from sunup until sundown to make money. But he earned only enough to feed his family.

The moneylender looked at his books. "Danh Nguyen has not paid me what he owes," he thought. "I am tired of waiting. I am tired of being nice. I will collect that money today, or I will take his fishing boat."

He went to the peasant's house and rapped loudly on the door.

"Come in," called a little voice.

The moneylender pushed the door open. There sat Lan, the fisherman's eight-year-old daughter. She was weaving a bamboo mat.

"Where are your parents, girl?" boomed the rich man's voice.

Lan did not answer. She did not even look up.

"Hey, child. I am talking to you. Where are your parents?" repeated the rich man.

"They are not here," she answered quietly.

"Well, where are they, then?" he demanded.

The young girl looked up at the rich man. Finally she spoke. "My father is catching fish so he can sell their bones. My mother is in the marketplace selling the wind."

"What?" cried the moneylender. "Do you think I'm crazy? What kind of an answer is that? You had better think twice before you play games with me!"

But no matter how the rich man stormed, Lan's reply was always the same.

The moneylender huffed and puffed in anger. His face grew red. "See here," he cried. "I have come to cancel your parents' debts. That is why I am here. But how can I give them the news if you won't tell me where they are? Where are they hiding? Tell them to come out."

"They are not hiding, sir. And it is you who has played games. Your promise is not real."

"By the blue sky above, my promise is real," said the moneylender.

"If your promise is real, then I will tell you where they are," said Lan. "But I will need a witness. The blue sky cannot be my witness. I must have a living being."

"But there is no one here except you and me," said the rich man.

"Well, there is that fly there upon the wall," said Lan. "It can be my witness."

"Fine!" said the moneylender. "A fine witness!" But he thought to himself, "What a stupid little girl."

"Sir," Lan began, "my father is away fishing, just as I said. We will eat the fish he catches. But with the bones my father will make hooks and needles. He will sell them in the village. And my mother is in the village now. She is selling fans. Wouldn't you say that she is selling the wind?"

The moneylender chuckled. He had to admit that the girl was more clever than he first thought. But he planned to return the next day for his money. "A fly as a witness! How ridiculous!" he thought to himself.

That night Lan told her parents all that had happened. She said the moneylender would come in person to give them the news.

The moneylender came back the next day. But he did not have good news. He demanded his money.

"Wait," said Lan's father. "You have made a promise to our daughter. You have promised you would cancel our debts."

"You must be crazy! I would never cancel your debts. Your daughter is lying," said the rich man.

"My daughter does not lie. We will let the mandarin decide," said Danh Nguyen.

"Well, there is that fly there upon the wall," said Lan. "It can be my witness."

The next day, the mandarin heard the rich man's story. Then he heard the poor man's story. Finally, he turned to the girl. "And what do you have to say? Do you have any proof that this man has cancelled your parents' debts?"

"Yes, I do," replied Lan. "I have a witness."

"Bring him forward," said the mandarin.

"It is that fly there, the one on the back of your chair," said the girl.

The mandarin became angry. He turned to Lan's parents. "I should make you pay a fine," he said. "Your daughter has wasted the court's time."

Lan jumped from her seat. "No, sir, I am telling the truth! The fly was there, right on the end of the moneylender's nose!"

This time the rich man jumped from his seat. "It was not on my nose!" he shouted. "It was on the wall!"

As soon as he spoke the words, the moneylender knew what he had done. But it was too late.

The mandarin laughed. The audience in the courtroom laughed. The girl and her parents laughed. Even the moneylender had to laugh.

The mandarin turned to the moneylender. "You, sir," he said, "have made a promise after all. I order that you keep it."

And with that, he dismissed everyone from his court.

IT'S THE SAME OLD STORY

Building Reading Comprehension

Part 1

The sentences below tell the story of "The Witness." But the sentences are all mixed up. Put the sentences in the right order.

Chanh	stayed	poor	collect	sister	beggar	give	to
playing	son	city	alms	he	stupid	loved	his

He went to <u>collect</u> money <u>from</u> Danh Nguyen. <u>She</u> was very <u>clever</u>. A <u>rich</u> <u>moneylender</u> lived in the <u>village</u>. Danh Nguyen and his wife were <u>working</u>. Everyone <u>hated</u> him. <u>She</u> made the <u>moneylender</u> promise to <u>cancel</u> <u>her</u> parents' debts. <u>Lan</u> was Danh's <u>daughter</u>.

_____

_____

_____

_____

_____

_____

Part 2

Some of the words in the sentences above are underlined. Replace the underlined words with an opposite word from the list. Now rewrite the story with the new words. Is the story different? Be able to discuss how.

_____

_____

_____

_____

_____

_____

AS PROUD AS A PEACOCK

Building Story Interpretation

Lan, the girl in the story, said that her mother had gone to the marketplace to sell the wind. That was an imaginative way to say that her mother was selling fans.

Read these phrases. They are an imaginative way to tell what someone is like or how someone does something.

as sly as a fox	like a volcano	as stubborn as a mule
works like a horse	cried like a baby	as proud as a peacock
as flat as a pancake	as fast as the wind	as strong as an ox
like sunshine	as hot as an oven	cut like a knife
trembled like a colt	eats like a pig	as powerful as a locomotive

Choose one of the phrases above to complete each sentence.

1. When her new car was in an accident, she _____

   _____.

2. The moneylender is fat because he _____.

3. The strong wind against her skin _____.

4. He has been training at the gym. Now he is_____

   _____.

5. In the summertime, this room gets _____.

6. Her smile makes everyone happy. She is _____

   _____on a cloudy day.

7. He never misses a day on the job, and he always _____

   _____.

8. He has a very short temper. When he gets angry, he explodes _____

   _____.

JUST A FLY ON THE WALL

Building Creative Thinking

Write on any of the following activities:

- Pretend you are a fly. Write about your life. What do you do throughout the day? Where do you go, what do you see, what do you eat? Who are your enemies? What do you do to avoid them? Where do you live, what are your biggest problems, etc.

- Lan's parents win the case and their debts are cancelled. But what happens next in the story? Write the next chapter from
  - a) the moneylender's viewpoint; or
  - b) Lan's parent's viewpoint; or
  - c) Lan's viewpoint

- Pick any five of the similes from the exercise on the previous page. Write sentences for them.

_____

_____

_____

_____

_____

_____

_____

_____

_____

_____

_____

Building Grammar and Syntax

Look at these sentences. Discover the rule.

> Last summer I went to Brazil.
> I have gone to Brazil many times.

> You worked hard on that job.
> You have worked hard on every job you have had.

> She sang in the choir last Sunday.
> She often has sung in the choir.

Make sentences using the words in parentheses. Use the has / have + -ed *form.*

1. (moneylender / always / live / in that village)

_____

2. (no one / ever / like / him)

_____

3. (he / always / charge / the highest interest rates)

_____

4. (he / never / need / any more money)

_____

5. (for several years / he / want / more than anyone else)

_____

6. (Danh Nguyen / owe / the money / for a long time)

_____

7. (moneylender / demand / payment / for the last time)

_____

Building Vocabulary

Look at the list of expressions on page 39.

For each one, draw a picture showing what it means, or write a short definition. Work alone, with a partner, or in small groups.

THE STOLEN SON

n a faraway kingdom lived a king and queen. They had no children. The queen wished and prayed each night for a son or a daughter.

One night the queen had a strange dream. A fairy appeared to her, saying, "You shall have a son. He will have a gift worth more than gold. Whatever he wishes for, he shall have. Tell no one about this dream. Tell no one about your son's gift."

In the morning, the king and queen were having breakfast. The queen remembered her dream, but she forgot to keep it a secret. She told her husband the dream, she told her maid, she told the cook in the kitchen.

The cook thought, "This is an unusual dream. Let's see if it comes true."

Sure enough, within the year, a beautiful prince was born. The queen's happiness was greater than words could tell. She spent every waking minute with her child.

Each day, the queen took her infant son for a walk. She strolled through the gardens and sang lullabies. She walked along the path to a stream that ran past the castle. There she would lay down a blanket. She would sing and rock her child to sleep, and then she would fall asleep next to him.

The cook watched all this. He talked to the maid. The two of them made a terrible plan.

The maid took the young prince's clothes and toys to a small shack in the woods. Then she waited.

The cook killed a chicken. He followed the queen down to the stream. When he was sure she was asleep, he spilled the chicken's blood on the queen's clothes and on the blanket. Quietly, carefully, he lifted the sleeping prince from his mother's arms. He took the prince to the maid and then returned to the palace. There, he ran to the king. He cried, "Your majesty, the queen fell asleep with the baby and allowed wild animals to eat him! Come quickly!"

The king followed the cook down to the stream. There was the queen, fast asleep. She was covered with blood. The blanket was covered with blood. The baby was nowhere to be found.

The king's wail shook the forest. The queen awoke. When she saw that her baby was gone, her tears could have filled an ocean. But her tears and grief did not soften the king's heart. His anger towards the queen was great. He ordered a tower to be built. He had the queen locked in the tower. He ordered that she be given nothing to eat or drink but bread and water. He thought that in a short time she would starve to death.

But good fairies watched over the queen. Every day, they sent doves to the queen. The doves brought fruit and meat and milk and honey. And so the queen lived on. Her heart was broken, but she lived.

The cook and the maid took care of the prince. When he was old enough to think and to speak, they knew he was ready to make wishes. They would say, "Don't you wish you had a fine palace to live in? Don't you wish we had cellars full of gold and silver?"

The little prince would say yes, and the cook and the maid became rich and fat and happy.

Years passed. The cook had everything he wanted. He began to worry about the prince, who was now a young man. He spoke to the maid.

"We must do something about this prince. He will destroy us. What if he should travel? What if he should wish to be with his parents? He would find out who we really are. You must kill him. Cut out his heart and bring it to me in the morning."

"Why must I kill him?" thought the maid. "He has given us everything. He has hurt no one. I cannot do it."

In the morning, she woke the prince. She told him who he really was. She told him about his wonderful gift. "Now," she said, "you must leave at once. Your life is in danger. Do not ask questions. Just go."

The prince pretended to go. But he sneaked back into the palace of his false parents and hid in a closet.

The maid hunted a deer, killed it, and took out its heart to give to the wicked cook. The prince watched. When the cook received the heart of the deer, the young man jumped from the closet. "You are evil!" he cried. "You do not deserve to be a man! Be a dog! My poor mother has had to eat only

The prince spoke the words. The cook became a large black dog.

bread and water. You shall eat ashes!"

The prince spoke the words. The cook became a large black dog.

"I wish to see my mother!" said the prince. He found himself instantly in the tower. "I want my father here!" he called. And the king appeared. "You, sir, should be locked up here, not my mother," said the prince to his father. "Wild animals never harmed me. Your cook stole me from the arms of my mother. He pretended to be my father and became rich with me as his son. Now he is this dog. I want you to see who he really is."

At that moment, the dog turned back into the cook. He stood trembling before the king.

"He was better as a dog," said the king. "Turn him back into a dog." Then the king wept. He begged his wife to forgive him. He embraced his son.

The three returned to the palace, with the black dog at their side. In time, the prince became king. He ruled wisely and well. But the cook remained a dog until his dying day. And he ate ashes until his tongue turned black.

WHO DOES THIS BELONG TO?

Building Reading Comprehension

Match the characters with the things that belong to them.

a soft blanket	a kingdom	a dead chicken
great anger	an evil heart	tears to fill an ocean
a hard heart	a loving mother	an accomplice
a dream	false parents	a leash
magical powers	a wife	breakfast
bread and water	a rattle	a baby
a knife	a broken heart	

the queen

_____

_____

_____

_____

_____

the king

_____

_____

_____

_____

_____

the prince

_____

_____

_____

_____

_____

the cook

_____

_____

_____

_____

_____

KIDNAPPED!

Building Story Interpretation

The queen knows her baby was not eaten by wild animals. She knows he was kidnapped. She posts notices all over the kingdom. What does she say?

Work alone, with a partner, or in a small group. Write your notice on this page, or develop an art project.

HEAR YE! HEAR YE!

Building Creative Thinking

On your own paper, write on any of the following activities.

- The queen goes before the people. She asks their help in finding her son. Write her speech. She must tell the people where she was and what she was doing at the time of the kidnapping; who the suspects are, if any; and any descriptions. Have her tell the people what the king will do to her if the young prince is not returned.

- The prince has returned as a young man. The family is reunited, but not for long. The queen is furious with her husband. She thinks his treatment of her was unfair. She leaves the kingdom. From her new home, she writes the king a letter. What does she say?

- You are the cook/dog. Convince the prince that you should not have to remain a dog for the rest of your life.

- You can make three wishes for yourself. (One of them cannot be to have infinite wishes.) What are your wishes? Why?

- You can make three wishes for the world. What are they? Explain.

DIDN'T, DON'T, CAN'T, WON'T

Building Grammar and Syntax

Look at the list. Discover the rule.

are not = aren't	is not = isn't	was not = wasn't
were not = weren't	cannot = can't	will not = won't
do not = don't	does not = doesn't	did not = didn't
have not = haven't	has not = hasn't	had not = hadn't
could not = couldn't	should not = shouldn't	would not = wouldn't

Complete each sentence with a contraction from the list. Use the story to help you.

1. The king and queen _____ any children.

2. The fairy said, "You _____ have a daughter; you will have a son."

3. The fairy said, "_____ tell anyone about this dream."

4. The queen _____ keep the dream a secret.

5. The queen _____ have been happier.

6. The cook _____ kill a duck. He killed a chicken.

7. The queen _____ covered with a blanket. She was covered with blood.

8. The queen _____ have fallen asleep.

9. The baby _____ anywhere to be found.

10. The cook and the maid _____ planning to do good. They were planning to do evil.

11. The cook and the maid said, "_____ you want cellars full of gold and silver?"

12. The cook said, "We _____ allow the prince to live. You must kill him."

IT'S A PUZZLE TO ME

Building Vocabulary

Complete the crossword puzzle.

ACROSS
1. The king's wife
2. 24 months
3. What's left after wood burns .
4. Not rich
5. A collie, for one
6. Having great wealth
7. A child's cover
8. To want or desire
9. A police officer's job is filled with _____.

DOWN
1. Without a sound
2. Not day
3. Not awake
4. Whole wheat _____
5. The earth, or soil
6. From the _____, the air traffic controller directed the plane.

THE FEATHER-MAIDEN

 ld Korush was a wicked sorcerer. He had made himself a magic sack, and with it he got whatever he wanted. He had only to say, "Snickety-snack, take your place in my sack," and whatever it was was forced to hop inside.

Korush decided it was time to marry. He disguised himself as a beggar and went from house to house. When a beautiful maiden came to the door, he would say, "Snickety-snack, take your place in my sack." He would then carry her off to his castle in the woods.

Korush came at last to the home of a rich merchant. The merchant had three beautiful daughters, Sidonia, Secunda, and Selene. Korush knocked, and the eldest daughter answered. She offered him bread and beer. He opened the sack as if to take it, but then touched the girl's arm and said, "Snickety-snack, take your place in my sack!" Girl, bread, and beer were forced to hop inside, and Korush carted them off to the woods as fast as he could go.

Inside the castle, the sorcerer let the frightened girl out of the sack. "I'm sorry I had to trick you, my dear Sidonia. But it was the only way to get you to come. All that I have can be yours. Look around. See if you like it here."

For two days, the merchant's daughter strolled through the wizard's castle and gardens. Never had she seen so many treasures. On the third day, the wizard brought her a set of keys and an egg. He said, "I must take a trip.

Here are the keys to the rooms in the tower. You may explore all of them but one. You may not go into the room at the end of the hallway. If you value your life, do not open the door to that room. Take this egg. Keep it safe. It will protect you from harm."

Korush left, and Sidonia was left alone. She climbed the long circle of stairs to the tower. At the top, she found herself in a long corridor. There were locked doors on both sides. At the very end was a tiny little door locked with a padlock. Sidonia began to go through the rooms, one by one. Each one was more magnificent than the one before.

She passed by the tiny door with the iron padlock, once, twice, three times, four times. Her curiosity grew and grew. She wanted to know what was behind that door. She found the smallest key and fit it into the lock. *Click!* The lock opened and fell to the ground. The maiden took the egg out of her apron pocket. "I will hold this," she thought. "The wizard said it would keep me safe from harm." Sidonia pushed the door open with her foot. The opening to the room was very, very small. Dropping to her hands and knees, the maiden crawled through the doorway.

Inside the room the light was very dim. The merchant's daughter could see shadows but could not see form. She felt something on the floor, though—something thick and wet. Little by little, she began to see something in that dim light. What she saw made the blood of her heart run cold. All around the room, chained to the walls, were the bloodstained bodies of young women. Blood covered the floor of the room.

Sidonia covered her face with her hands and screamed. In her terror, she dropped the egg to the ground. When she picked it up, it was covered with blood. She ran from the room and locked the door behind her. She tried to wipe the blood from the egg, but it would not come off. She rinsed the egg, she washed it, she scrubbed it, and she rubbed it. But no matter what, the blood stuck like glue.

The sorcerer returned in the evening. He asked for the keys and the egg. When he saw the bloodstained egg he exclaimed, "Ah, madame, you tried to hatch the egg too soon! You disobeyed me. Now you will take your place on the wall along with all the rest." He took her to the forbidden room and chained her to the wall.

The following day, he returned to the merchant's house. Secunda came to the door. She was snatched away just as her older sister had been. And in the sorcerer's castle, everything happened with the second sister as had happened with the first. The maiden wound up chained to a hook beside her sister.

The sorcerer went for a third time to the merchant's house and came away with the youngest daughter, Selene, in his sack. He gave her the keys and the egg. He warned her about opening the forbidden door, and then he went on his way.

So Korush struggled on, thinking that his bride-to-be was watching.

Selene was very clever. She took the egg out to the henhouse. "The safest place for you," she said, "is with your mother." She found a hen sitting on its nest and tucked the egg under its soft, warm feathers. Then she climbed the spiral staircase to the tower. She wasted no time exploring the sorcerer's treasures, but went straight to the forbidden door and opened it. Inside, she found her sisters hanging from the wall. Both were nearly dead.

She unchained them and carried them out of the tower. After giving them food and drink, she spoke. "I will have a chance to save you. Do as I say. Say what I tell you to say. All will be well."

She hid her sisters in the woodshed. She took the egg from beneath the hen and waited for the wizard's return.

When Korush entered, he asked for the keys and the egg. He looked at the egg carefully. Finding it clean, he said, "You have passed the test. You shall be my bride."

"But what gift will you give my parents?" asked the merchant's youngest daughter.

"What gift do you want me to give?" answered the sorcerer.

"Only this. I will fill a large sack with gold. Carry it by yourself, on your back, to my parents. Use no magic. I will watch from the window to see that you do not stop along the way."

"Done!" said the wizard.

The maiden had her two sisters creep into the sack. She covered them with gold. Korush started off. The sack was very heavy. "I must rest," he said to himself. But a voice from inside the sack said, "If you want me as your bride, you must not stop." So Korush struggled on, thinking that his bride-to-be was watching.

Selene found the egg and cracked it open. The white of the egg poured out in a stream of glossy white feathers. The yolk poured out as a pool of golden honey. The maiden rolled herself from head to toe in the honey. Then she rolled herself in the feathers. She looked like a beautiful white bird. She started off down the road.

Each person she met along the way asked, "How goes the young bride? When will the wedding be?"

"She is preparing the wedding feast. She will call for you soon," answered the feather-maiden.

At last she met old Korush, returning from her parents' house.

"Have you seen my bride? Is she as beautiful as a white bird?" asked the wizard.

"Yes, she is. And she is waiting for you inside," answered the feather-maiden.

Korush hurried off to his castle. The feather-maiden followed along behind. When the old sorcerer was safely inside the walls of the castle, the feather-maiden locked every gate all around.

She then set fire to the castle and watched as it burned slowly to the ground. From the dying flames, the feather-maiden heard a squawk and the flutter of wings. She looked and saw one black crow rise from the coals. It flew to the west, toward the setting sun. The feather-maiden returned to her home.

IT'S ALL IN A DAY'S WORK

Building Reading Comprehension

You are a private investigator. The rich merchant of our story hires you. "My daughters are missing," he tells you. "Find them, and I'll make you a rich man."

On another piece of paper, retrace the evil sorcerer's steps. Illustrate the events of the story in any way you or your group decides. Label each event with a short sentence.

WANTED, DEAD OR ALIVE!!

Building Story Interpretation

Your investigation has taken you right to the gate of Korush's castle. But you can't get inside to rescue the maidens. Korush has cast a spell over the gate. The king of the land wants this sorcerer caught. He has offered a huge reward.

On your own paper, write on one of the following:

- Some of the people want the king dethroned. Their daughters are disappearing and they don't think the king has done enough to solve the mystery. You are the prime minister. You would like to become king. Write a speech. Go before the people. Talk about the king and why he should be dethroned. Talk about yourself. Why would you make a better king? Tell the people your plan of action to find the missing maidens and to capture the sorcerer.

- You are the king. Make a poster offering a reward for Korush's capture. Describe the sorcerer, tell where he lives and where he was last seen. Give any information about his habits. What disguises has he used? When does he leave his castle? When is he usually in town?

- You are the sorcerer. Write the magic spell that you used to seal the castle.

- You are the investigator. You know more about when Korush comes and goes than anyone else. Write the information that you have about the sorcerer. Make a plan for his capture.

- You are a wizard who does only good. Write a spell to unlock Korush's gates. Write another to turn him into a crow.

WHAT HAPPENS NEXT?

Building Creative Thinking

The story "The Feather-Maiden" does not really end. Think of one possibility for the next chapter and write it. You may work alone, with a partner, or in a small group.

_____

_____

_____

_____

_____

_____

_____

_____

_____

_____

_____

_____

_____

_____

_____

_____

WHERE IS IT?

Building Grammar and Syntax

In each phrase, underline the preposition. It will be the word that tells you where.

1. walked into the room

2. in the sack

3. ran to the castle

4. across the bridge

5. strolled through the gardens

6. crawled through the doorway

7. hanging on the wall

8. fell to the ground

9. something on the floor

10. above the castle

11. behind the door

12. down the road

13. under the hen

14. over the tower

15. rose from the ashes

SAME OR DIFFERENT?

Building Vocabulary

Write words that mean the same and the opposite for each word given below. Choose words from the list.

evil	run	sweet	start	pull	fasten	nice	unlock
lovely	huge	fall	shove	walk	end	ugly	smart
rush	mean	ask	go up	wife	good	fair	tap
small	groom	close	reply	stupid	cute	unfasten	

	SAME		**OPPOSITE**
wicked	_____	wicked	_____
beautiful	_____	beautiful	_____
stroll	_____	stroll	_____
open	_____	open	_____
begin	_____	begin	_____
tiny	_____	tiny	_____
push	_____	push	_____
rise	_____	rise	_____
lock	_____	lock	_____
clever	_____	clever	_____
bride	_____	bride	_____
answer	_____	answer	_____

THE
GODFATHER

here once was a poor woodcarver. He had more children than he had fingers to count them. A thirteenth child was born. The poor man went outside, sat on a stump, and wept.

"Thirteen is unlucky," he sobbed. "I shall never find a god-father for my child."

By and by, along came a very old man. He was as thin as paper.

His bones rattled and clacked as he walked. His skin was wrinkled and brown with age. He stopped in front of the woodcarver. "Why do you weep?" he asked. "You are young and full of life."

"I am sad and unlucky," answered the woodcarver. "My thirteenth child was born this morning. Thirteen is unlucky. No one will want to be his god-father."

"Take me for the godfather," said the old man.

"But who are you? I don't even know you," replied the father.

"You know me," said the old man. "I took your brother's wife last winter. I took your wife's mother two years ago. I took the mayor in October. I am Death. I treat all persons equally. Take me for your son's godfather. With me as his friend, he can have a great life."

Death became the boy's godfather. On the boy's thirteenth birthday, Death came for him.

"I am your godfather," he said. "You must come with me. It is time for you to learn about life."

He led the boy into a great forest. "Look around. Choose what you like. Choose carefully. You are choosing your own future."

"This is odd," thought the boy. "Here is a rock, there a vine, there a bit of moss. My godfather is giving me a strange gift."

But the boy looked around. He looked carefully. His eye fell on a plant. It had long, shiny green leaves. In the heart of the plant was one blood-red flower. The boy could not take his eye from the plant.

"I choose this," he said at last.

"This is the plant of the physician," said his godfather. "You will become a great physician. I will teach you all you need to know."

One day, Death called his godson to his side. "You are ready," he said. "Listen carefully. When you are called to take care of the sick, look for me. I will always appear. If I stand at the head of the bed, you may do your work. Give the person medicine made from the plant. Their health will return immediately. But if I stand at the foot of the bed, the person is mine. Do not use the plant against me. Now go."

In a very short time, the young man did become the greatest physician in the land. He became famous. People came from all over the world for his treatment. They paid him great amounts of money. He became rich—very rich and very proud.

One day, the king's messenger called for the physician. "Come quickly," he said. "Our king is very ill."

The physician went to the king's bedside. He was weak and pale. At the foot of the bed stood Death.

"My godfather is getting too old for his job," thought the physician. "I saw the king yesterday. He was well and strong. Surely my godfather will see his mistake. And the king will make me a great lord."

The physician walked over to the bed and turned it around. The head now stood where the foot had been. Color returned to the king's face. The physician gave the king a bit of the plant. The king sat up, completely cured.

The next day, Death paid his godson a visit. He was very angry. "Once, I will let you cheat me, because you are my godson. But do not think you can cheat me again."

Several months later, the physician again was called to the king's palace. He was taken to the bedside of the princess.

"She is my only child," said the king. "Save her and she shall be your bride."

The physician looked at the sleeping princess. She was beautiful. "The princess shall be my bride, and one day I shall be king," he thought.

Just then, Death appeared. He looked sternly at his godson, and then walked to the foot of the princess's bed.

The physician looked at his godfather. He shook his head. He lifted up

Death led his godson to a tiny candle. Its flame was dying.

the princess and turned her around. Her head now lay at the foot of the bed. Color returned to her cheeks, and she opened her eyes. The physician gave her a potion made from the plant. She sat up and was cured.

That night, the door to the physician's bedroom opened. In hobbled godfather Death. He gripped his godson's shoulder with a bony hand. "Come with me," he said.

Down, down, down into the underworld they went. There the physician saw rows upon rows of candles. Some were tall, with bright flames. Some were tiny, with almost no flame at all. Every moment, the fires of some candles went out. At the same moment, new candles were lit.

Death spoke. "Do you see? These are the lights of men's lives. Some of the smallest belong to old men. But some belong to young children. You think you know which flames should die. But you do not."

"Do I have a candle?" asked the physician.

"Are you not a man?" answered Death.

"Show me. Show me my candle," begged the physician.

Death led his godson to a tiny candle. Its flame was dying.

"Ah, no!" cried the physician. "Light a new one for me."

"I cannot," answered Death. "Yesterday this candle was tall. Its flame was bright. But you choose wrongly. You made the candle burn fast. I can do nothing."

"Please—!" cried the physician.

At that moment, the flame of the physician's candle went out. He spoke no more.

THAT'S AN ORDER!

Building Reading Comprehension

These sentences from the story are in the wrong order. Write them in the correct order. When you are finished, you will have a paragraph that summarizes the story.

He became the child's godfather. The physician became proud. He saved the king and the princess. There, he saw the flames of mens' lives. A woodcarver had many children. A thin, bony old man came walking along the road. He would not follow Death's instructions. They should have died. The thin, bony old man was Death. He understood the meaning of life, but too late. He could not find a godfather for his thirteenth child. He taught his godson to become a physician. Death took his godson to the underworld. His own flame went out and he died.

_____

_____

_____

_____

_____

_____

_____

_____

_____

_____

_____

HOUSE CALL

Building Story Interpretation

You are ill. The physician is called to your home. Describe your symptoms in clear detail. Use the words and phrases to help you.

sore throat	headache	aspirin	every four hours
operation	diet	fever	trouble breathing
no appetite	runny nose	decongestant	plenty of fluids
daily exercise	vitamins	plenty of rest	back pain
rash	blisters	dizzy	a stomach ache
sneezing	tired	cough	earache

Patient: _____

_____

_____

_____

_____

_____

Now take the role of the physician. Write out your prescription for your patient.

Doctor: _____

_____

_____

_____

_____

_____

NO SECOND CHANCE

Building Creative Thinking

On your own paper, write on any one of the following situations:

- You are the physician, and you are in the underworld. You want your godfather to give you another chance to live. What do you say to convince him? List all your arguments in a letter to your godfather.

- You are godfather Death. You have read your godson's letter, and you decide to give him a second chance. Write him a letter telling him why you will give him this chance. But he will have to do something to prove that he should have this chance. When he is back on earth, what tasks will he have to do?

- You are the editor of the kingdom's newspaper. The king and princess should have died. They didn't because the physician interfered. Write a newspaper article. Describe the problems that have happened because of what the physician did. Tell what would have happened if he had not interfered. How would the world be different?

- Your best friend learns suddenly that he or she must move to the other side of the world. You will probably never see each other again. This is your last chance to tell your friend how important the friendship has been. Write your thoughts in a letter.

Building Grammar and Syntax

How do you show that something belongs to someone, or something else?

Do it like this:

the gift of the physician = the physician's gift
the heart of the plant = the plant's heart
the children of my father = my father's children
the dresses of the ladies = the ladies' dresses
the house of my parents = my parents' house
the godfathers of the children = the children's godfathers

Rewrite this story on your own paper. Change the underlined word or phrase to the 's form.

Koum (Death) and Ammi

There once was a village in Africa named Diguila. The people of Diguila did not know sleep or death.

The most beautiful maiden of Diguila was Ammi. The beauty of Ammi was known throughout the land.

All the young men wanted to marry Ammi, but Ammi loved only Koum.

Koum lived in a village called Daoda. He was the chief of Daoda. The name of Koum meant "Death." Koum was a powerful sorcerer, but Ammi did not know this.

Ammi and Koum were married. The happiness of the couple was great.

The happiness of Ammi was greater when she learned she would have a baby.

But soon her joy turned to sorrow. A servant told her, "The powers of your husband are terrible. He can take the living and make them stiff and lifeless."

Ammi was frightened. In the dark of the night, she stole away to the village of her father. There she gave birth to four baby boys. They were strong and beautiful. But they did something that no one had ever seen before. They slept. The fear of the villagers was great.

The sons of Ammi grew. The magical powers of the boys grew, too. The village priests could do nothing. None of the magic spells of the priests worked against the magic of the boys. One day these young sorcerers decided to test their powers. They decided to put the people of the village to death. But they had only inherited half of the powers of their father. The most they could do was make everyone fall asleep at the end of the day.

FAMILY TIES

Building Vocabulary

Rewrite each sentence. Change the words in parentheses to one of the words in the box. Use a dictionary to help you. Work in pairs or teams.

mother	sister	brother	mother-in-law
father-in-law	brother-in-law	son-in-law	aunt
uncle	niece	nephew	cousin
stepmother	stepfather	grandmother	great-grandmother

1. My (mother's mother's mother) lived in Norway.

   _____

2. My (one of my parents' children; a girl) now lives in Los Angeles.

   _____

3. Maria's (the son or daughter of her uncle or aunt) will be eighteen years old in June.

   _____

4. My (husband's mother) is coming for a short visit.

   _____

5. The physician's (mother's mother or father's mother) died in October.

   _____

6. Chuyen's (father's sister or mother's sister) is an airplane pilot.

   _____

7. My (sister's husband) works with computers.

   _____

8. Cinderella's (father's new wife) was mean and cruel.

   _____

wo brothers traveled along together. One was rich and the other was poor. The rich brother rode in a fine cart pulled by a strong gelding. The poor brother had only a sweet-tempered mare.

The two men came to a fork in the road. It was nighttime, and they could not tell which way to go.

"We shall spend the night here," said the rich man, pointing to a brightly lit inn at the side of the road.

He got out of his cart and went inside. Sounds of laughter and music filled the air. The poor brother slept outside under a tree.

During the night, the mare give birth to a foal, and it rolled under the rich man's cart. When he came out of the inn in the morning, he shook his younger brother awake. "I declare," he exclaimed. "Will you look at this! My cart has given birth to a fine little foal!"

The younger brother sat up and rubbed his eyes. "Don't be ridiculous!" he cried. "Carts do not bear foals. Mares bear foals. It was my mare that bore the foal."

"If that were so," snapped the first, "your mare would have her baby by her side. The foal belongs to the cart, the cart belongs to me, and the foal does, too."

The two began to argue, and then to shout. Before long, a crowd had gathered.

"Before there's a fight," said one of the crowd, "take your case to the magistrate."

And so the two did just that. But the magistrate could not decide, and so he sent the case along to the king. The king could not decide, either. But since he was the king, he knew he must. "The foal was found with the cart," declared the king. "The foal shall remain with the cart."

The king spoke the words, but the poor man could not believe his ears. He left the court muttering horrible things about the king. By the time he reached the courtyard next to the royal garden, he was shouting and stomping his feet. The queen happened to be out gathering flowers and heard the commotion.

"What are you doing?" she asked. "And what, pray tell, is the matter? Why are you so angry?"

"Your husband," replied the poor man, "is an idiot. He believes that carts bear foals."

"Oh?" replied the queen. "What gives you that idea?"

The poor brother told her the whole story and ended by asking for her help.

Now, the queen was known to be very clever. "I will help you," she said. "You have only to do what I say, and you will win back your little foal. Tomorrow the king will go walking along this very path. Up ahead there is a pond, but it is bone dry. Go there tomorrow with a fishing pole and pretend to fish. When the king passes by, he will question you. Give him the answer that I will tell you now."

Well, the next day the younger brother was there at the pond with his fishing pole. He waited and waited. At last he saw the king coming. He cast his line into the dry pond and after a moment jerked it wildly up and down. "Whoa-ho-ho!" he shouted. "This is a BIG one!"

The king watched in amazement. At last he spoke. "Hey there! Just what do you think you're doing?"

"Why, I'm fishing, your majesty. Can't you see?" answered the peasant.

"Fishing for what?" asked the king. "Rocks?"

"Fish," the young man said simply.

The king roared with laughter. "Fish on," he bellowed. "Fish for a thousand years." Shaking his head, he started to walk away. "Only a moron would think he could catch fish from a dry pond."

"Majesty," called the poor man, "if a cart can give birth to a foal, I should have no trouble at all catching fish from a dry pond."

At this, the king's servants burst into laughter. The king's face turned red, and he stopped. "INTO MY CHAMBERS!" he roared.

As they approached his castle, the king said, "I will change my decision

"Your husband," replied the poor man, *"is an idiot."*

on one condition. You did not think of this plan alone. Tell me who helped you, and the colt is yours."

The peasant did not want to get the queen in trouble, but he wanted his colt. At last he told the king all that had happened.

When the poor man had gone, the king called his wife to him. "Catherine," he said, "I have warned you about meddling in state business, but you refuse to obey me. This time you have gone too far. I have been embarrassed in front of my servants and a peasant. You can be my wife no longer. You must leave at once for your father's house. But I do not hate you. To prove that, I will give you a farewell gift. You may take from the castle the one thing you love best."

"Dear husband," replied the queen, "if this is your wish, I shall go. But at least give me this last evening with you. I will leave first thing in the morning."

"So be it," said the king.

The queen went right away to the royal kitchen. She ordered the cooks to prepare her husband's favorite foods. She had the best wines brought up from the cellar. She had flowers placed in the dining hall. Then she went to her dressing room, where she dressed herself in her most beautiful gown.

That night at dinner, she dismissed the servants. "I wish to serve you," she said as she poured the king a glass of wine. She bent down, kissed him on the cheek, and when he was not looking, slipped a sleeping potion into his drink.

"A toast to your health, Catherine, and your beauty," said the king. He took a big drink from his glass.

In a few minutes, the king had fallen fast asleep. The queen called the servants and had them take the sleeping king into a waiting carriage. She climbed in beside him and told the coachman to drive them to her father's house. There, she had him carried to her bed, where he slept for hours and hours.

When at last he awoke, he had no idea where he was. He called to his servants, but no one came. "CATHERINE!" he bellowed.

The door to the bedchamber opened. In walked the queen.

"What is the meaning of this?" cried the king. "Where am I?"

"You are in my father's house, my lord, and here you will stay. You promised me that I could take the one thing from the castle that I love best in the world. That is you."

These words brought tears of joy to the king's eyes. He chuckled softly and held his wife close to him. "Never," he whispered, "has there been another quite like you. Never again will we part."

They returned to the castle. From that day forward, the king never appeared in a court of justice without Catherine the Clever by his side.

ORDER IN THE COURT

Building Reading Comprehension

These events from the story are in the wrong order. Number them in the correct order.

_____ The poor brother tells the king that the queen helped him.

_____ The rich brother finds the foal under his cart.

_____ The cooks prepare the king's favorite dishes.

_____ The queen gives the poor brother advice.

_____ The queen orders the servants to take the king to her father's house.

_____ The king asks the poor brother if he is fishing for rocks.

_____ The magistrate sends the case to the king.

_____ The two brothers come to a fork in the road.

_____ The king awards the foal to the rich brother.

_____ The king changes his mind. He gives the foal to the poor brother.

DON'T GET LOST

Building Story Interpretation

Draw a map that shows all the main events of the story connected together with a path. The map can be any sort of map you want. Be creative! Next to the event write a short sentence telling what happened there.

Here is an example of how you might start.

The brothers come to a fork in the road.

LOST AND FOUND

Building Creative Thinking

Your prize Gemmel Bennis is missing. You post a sign describing it in detail and offering a reward. Use as many of the following as you can in your description: WHAT is it—is it animal, vegetable, or mineral? What is its name (if it has one)? How big is it or how small? What is its shape and color? What is it made of? Does it have moving parts or many parts? What is it used for or what does it do? Say where your Gemmel Bennis was last seen and why you must get it back.

Now have a partner draw your Gemmel Bennis from the description you have given. How well does his drawing match what you have written?

DON'T TENSE UP

Building Grammar and Syntax

Choose the correct form of the verb to complete each sentence.

1. Two brothers _____ along together.
   (traveling travels traveled)

2. One brother _____ rich. *(was be were)*

3. Both brothers _____ horses. *(has had have)*

4. The two men _____ to a fork in the road.
   (come comes came)

5. During the night, the mare _____ a foal.
   (bore bears bearing)

6. The foal _____ under the cart. *(roll rell rolled)*

7. The magistrate _____ the case to the king.
   (sends sended sent)

8. The king _____ the words.
   (spoke speaked spoken)

9. The poor man's mouth _____ open.
   (fallen felled fell)

10. The poor man _____ his feet.
    (stemp stomped stomps)

11. The poor man _____ the queen. *(sawed seed saw)*

12. The queen _____ the poor man advice.
    (gave giving gived)

13. The poor man _____ fishing in a dry pond.
    (goed going went)

14. The king _____ the man was crazy.
    (thinked thunk thought)

EVERYTHING IN ITS PLACE

Building Vocabulary

Choose words from the list to go with each title.

sign posts   worms   four legs   a hook   a master   a horse   rocks
a mane   old campsights   a carriage   a ruler   horseshoes   an inn   a reel
bait   vegetables   servants   weeds   a bucket   a throne   people waiting
a pole   a foal   a coat of arms   a lake   a strong man's shoulders
a watering can   a treasury   trees and bushes   a purse   confused travelers

"Things you find in a castle"

_____

_____

_____

_____

_____

"Things you see at a fork in the road"

_____

_____

_____

_____

_____

"Things a mare would have"

_____

_____

_____

_____

_____

"Things that carry other things"

_____

_____

_____

_____

_____

"Things you find in a garden"

_____

_____

_____

_____

_____

"Things that have to do with fishing"

_____

_____

_____

_____

_____

TOADS AND DIAMONDS

here once was a widow who had two daughters. The older daughter was the very mirror of her mother. Her face was always in a frown, she never had a kind word for anyone, and she was so bad-tempered that no one wanted to be around her. But her mother favored her, and treated her like a princess.

The younger daughter was as different from her sister as day is from night. Belle, as she was called, was as beautiful as a rose. Everyone said she was like her father, who had died years ago. She had a loving heart and a sweet temper. She was generous and kind. Everyone loved her—everyone except her own mother.

Belle's mother hated her. She gave her hard work to do from sunrise until sunset. In the winter, she sent her barefoot into the snow to find blackberries. (Of course, blackberries do not grow in the snow.) At night, she sent her deep into the forest to collect wood for the stove. (She hoped the wild animals would kill her.)

But Belle never was harmed. She did as her mother asked, and she always kept a gentle heart.

One day Belle's mother found an old wooden bucket. Its seams were split, and it had a hole in the middle. "This ought to do the trick," she thought.

She called her daughter to her side. "Take this bucket," she said, "and go down to the well. Fill the bucket to the rim. Do not let even one drop of water spill. Do not return home if the bucket is not completely full."

Belle looked at the bucket. She looked at its cracked sides and at the hole in the middle. "Ah," she thought, "my mother means to get rid of me for good." But she took the bucket and began to walk. No sooner had Belle arrived when an old woman came hobbling up. She asked the young woman to get her some water.

"This bucket does not look like it will hold a drop," said Belle, "but I will try."

She dipped the bucket into the clearest part of the well and raised it up. Much to her surprise, all the cracks had sealed and the hole had disappeared. Belle held the bucket for the old woman while she drank and drank and drank.

When the old woman was satisfied, she took the girl's hand. "You are as kind as you are beautiful," she said. "I have a gift for you. From this day forward, for every word you speak, a flower or a jewel shall fall from your mouth."

With that, the old woman (who was really a fairy) disappeared.

Belle filled her bucket again and hurried home. When her mother saw her, she said crossly, "You have taken a very long time. You shall go without dinner."

"I am sorry, Mother," said the girl, "but something amazing happened at the well."

Belle's mother watched in wonder as three diamonds, two roses, an orchid, and five pearls fell to the floor.

"My child!" she said, scooping up the gems. "What is happening here?"

Belle told her the whole story, and at the end of it, her mother had an apron full of riches.

The mother called to her other daughter. "Prunella, dear, look what gift your sister has gotten. You shall have it, too. All you have to do is go down to the well with this bucket. When an old woman asks you for water, give her some."

Now, Prunella did not like the idea of walking to the well. She took the finest horse in the stable. And she refused to take the wooden bucket. "Give me your silver pitcher," she said. "That way, if someone should see me, they will think I am drawing water for myself."

Seated atop her fine horse, Prunella arrived at the well within a short time. She waited throughout the day for an old woman to appear, asking for water, but no such woman appeared.

"This is a fine kettle of fish, indeed," thought Prunella. "Am I to sit out here and burn my fair skin FOREVER, waiting for some imaginary old woman to appear? I think NOT!" And she stood up and got ready to leave.

Scattered at her feet were gems and flowers of every sort.

At that moment she saw walking up the hill a beautiful woman, dressed like a queen, and followed by many servants. The woman walked over to the well and stopped. She looked at Prunella and at the pitcher in her hand. "I am thirsty," she said. "Will you draw me some water in that lovely pitcher of yours?"

Prunella scowled at the woman. "Do you think I am one of your servants?" she asked. "Get them to do it. Or do it yourself." And she tossed the pitcher in the direction of the lady.

The woman caught the pitcher. She dipped it into the well, raised it to her lips, and drank. All the while, she kept her eyes on Prunella.

When she had finished, she set the pitcher down. "You have the manners of a toad," she said simply. "And so I have a gift for you." (This was, you must have guessed, the same fairy who had appeared at the well earlier.) "My gift is this: From this day forward, for every word you speak, either a toad or viper shall slither from your lips." And then the fairy disappeared.

Prunella returned home. Her mother hurried out to greet her. "Well, my lovely daughter, how did it go?"

"Well, my dear mother, see for yourself," replied Prunella, and two toads, a salamander, a lizard, and three snakes fell from her mouth.

Prunella's mother screamed. "Your sister shall pay for this!" she cried.

Belle had seen everything from the window. Fearing her mother's anger, she ran from the house and hid herself deep in the woods. There she sobbed and sobbed.

The king's son was returning from a hunting trip. He heard the sobs. Following the sound, he came upon a beautiful young woman. Scattered at her feet were gems and flowers of every sort. He asked the young woman who she was and why she was so sad. He watched in amazement as she told her tale. By the end of the story, he was in love with her. He lifted her upon his horse and carried her to his father's palace. The king, seeing her wonderful gift, quickly gave his consent for the marriage. The two were wed, and the prince, in time, became king. With Belle at his side, he ruled wisely and was loved by his people.

And what about the sister, what happened to her? She had not been well liked before receiving her gift. After receiving it, she was hated and feared. Even her mother could not be near her.

She wandered about, looking for someone who would take care of her. When she found no one, she went deep into the woods. There she finally died.

DID IT HAPPEN? WHO DID IT?

Building Reading Comprehension

Read the sentences below. Some of the things happened in the story and some did not. Decide what happened and what did not. Write yes *or* no *on the first line. Think about who did it or could have done it. Write the character's name on the second line. The first one is done for you.*

	Did it happen?	**Who did it?**
1. She gave money to the poor	No	Belle
2. One of Belle's parents died.	_____	_____
3. She yelled at little children.	_____	_____
4. She never smiled.	_____	_____
5. She threw rocks at cats.	_____	_____
6. She treated one of her daughters like a princess.	_____	_____
7. She helped at the hospital without pay.	_____	_____
8. She made her daughter clean the chimney.	_____	_____
9. She collected wood in the forest.	_____	_____
10. She ate chocolate candies by the fireplace.	_____	_____
11. She found a wooden bucket.	_____	_____
12. She walked with a cane.	_____	_____
13. She drank much water.	_____	_____
14. She spoke, and perfume filled the air.	_____	_____

Building Story Interpretation

You can tell what someone is like, or how someone does something, by using the words like *or as . . . as.*

Make sentences using the clues below. Use the story to help you. Two sentences are done for you.

1. daughter / mirror / mother

The older daughter was like a mirror of her mother.

_____

2. her mouth / a toad's mouth

_____

_____

3. mother / treated / princess

_____

_____

4. Belle / beautiful / rose

Belle was as beautiful as a rose.

_____

5. heart / good / gold

_____

_____

6. mother / cruel / witch

_____

_____

7. blackberries / sweet / candy

_____

_____

8. his chair / old / wooden bucket

_____

_____

9. it / deep / well

_____

_____

YOUR WORDS ARE LIKE PEARLS

Building Creative Thinking

Choose any of the following activities. Write your ideas on your own paper.

- Belle finally has had enough of her mother's cruelty. She packs her bags and moves to town. (There she starts a business as a jeweler and a florist.) She writes her mother a letter. What might she say in that letter?

- In the story, the mother says to Prunella, "All you have to do is go down to the well with this bucket. When an old woman asks you for water, give her some." But the mother is forgetting some things. What else would Prunella have to do? How would she have to act? If she had drawn water for the lady, would she have gotten the same gift as Belle? Why or why not?

- Do you think the king's son was really in love with Belle? Why or why not?

- Imagine you have Belle's gift (or Prunella's, if you would rather). What kinds of problems could it cause in your life?

- Have you ever had a friend who liked you for what you had instead of for who you are? How did that feel? If that has never happened to you, imagine how it would feel. Write your thoughts.

- Have you ever liked someone for what they had instead of for who they are? Why or why not? What was the friendship like? How long did it last?

- Do you think Belle was right to take her mother's cruelty for so long? Why or why not? What could she have done in those days?

- Do you think people today have better manners or worse manners than in your grandmother's day? Why? What are the causes? What could you do to change things?

- What is one example of bad manners that you see every day? (Choose the thing that makes you the most angry.)

- Is there an excuse for being rude? Why or why not?

SOMEONE, ANYONE, NO ONE

Building Grammar and Syntax

Read these sentences. Discover the rule.

Someone left a message for Mr. Byfield.
Did anyone leave a message for Mr. Byfield?

That jewelry store is somewhere on Hill Street.
Is that jewelry store anywhere on Hill Street?

I have seen someone standing at the gate.
I haven't seen anyone standing at the gate.

Yolanda lost her purse somewhere on campus.
Yolanda didn't lose her purse anywhere on campus.

Choose someone, somebody, something, somewhere, anyone, anybody, anything, anywhere *to complete each sentence.*

1. _____ strange is happening in that village.

2. Belle saw _____ hobbling up to the well.

3. Can _____ tell me who that was?

   _____ must know.

4. Belle has never treated _____ unkindly.

5. Belle spoke, and _____ shiny fell out of her mouth.

6. Belle's mother didn't want _____ to know how cruel she was.

7. Prunella was lazy. She never did _____ to help her sister.

9. Has _____ ever found that well? Is it

   _____ on earth?

OPPOSITES ATTRACT

Building Vocabulary

Beside each word, write a word from the list that means the opposite or nearly the opposite.

soft	stingy	hate	smile	father	everyone
sour	laugh	ugly	take	never	received
sit	brother	tame	son	easy	younger
empty	same	cruel	shallow		

1. daughter _____

2. older _____

3. mother _____

4. always _____

5. frown _____

6. kind _____

7. no one _____

8. different _____

9. sister _____

10. beautiful _____

11. love _____

12. sweet _____

13. generous _____

14. hard _____

15. sent _____

16. deep _____

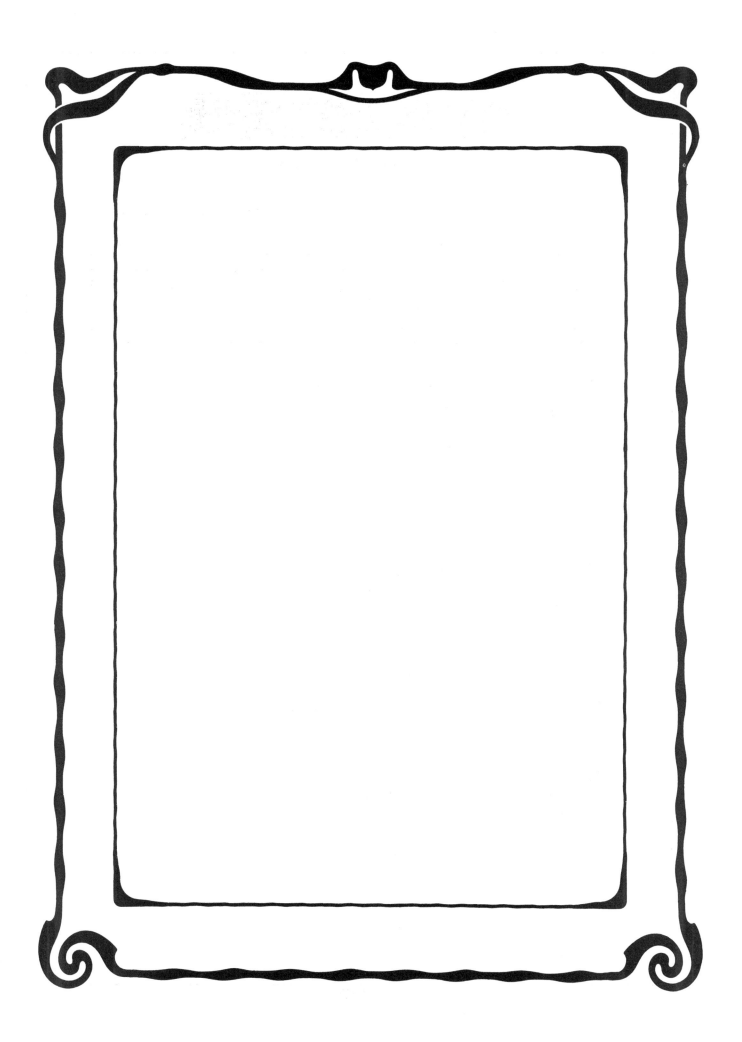